Roots of Rot and Ruin

Poetry for the lost and searching souls

Edgar J. Wilde

"I am the shadow cast by my own hand

A stranger in the mirror's gaze."

Introduction

Roots of Rot and Ruin began as a personal journey—an attempt to capture the darkest and rawest corners of my mind, a place where love and despair, hope and hurt, often coexist. Writing these poems felt like drawing a map of all the places I've wandered through in the search for meaning, for comfort, and, maybe, for a way to make peace with myself. This collection holds fragments of my own battles with addiction, self-worth, heartbreak, and the kind of love that consumes and scars. If you're here, perhaps you've felt those things too.

In these pages, you'll find a voice that sometimes wavers and often aches but speaks with unfiltered honesty. My words don't offer neat resolutions or easy answers—they reveal the struggle and surrender in trying to find light amid darkness, to hold onto hope while touching the edges of despair.

To those who find themselves reflected in these lines, know that you're not alone. Mental health struggles, addiction, heartbreak—these are battles that so many of us face in silence. I hope this collection brings you some sense of solidarity, a reminder that it's okay to feel broken sometimes, and that healing is often found in the rawest places.

Thank you for walking through these pages with me, for bearing witness to these parts of my soul. And above all, remember: You got this.

— Edgar J. Wilde

Dedication

For anyone that feels, even if you feel nothing.

Embrace the shadows, but remember, there's
light waiting when you're ready.

Acknowledgements

My parents, grandparents and those closest who have either inspired these words or supported me as I've felt the contents of these poems.

Of course, <u>the</u> one, who knows who they are. Three words.

Content Advisory

I usually don't subscribe to the idea of "trigger warnings," as I believe there's value in facing what makes us feel or react. Each encounter, uncomfortable as it may be, can help us build resilience. Shielding ourselves from discomfort can sometimes dull our capacity to cope, potentially doing more harm than good. That said, I am neither a doctor nor a psychiatrist, and I respect that everyone's journey is unique.

This collection explores themes of self-harm, suicide, love and loss, heartbreak, addiction, and self-worth. These poems aren't crafted for shock; they are simply reflections of my own feelings and experiences. I hope you'll continue to read, as growth often comes from stepping beyond the familiar and exploring what lies beyond our comfort zones.

Thank you for walking with me through these pages.

Contents

Section One: Love and Longing

Love begins like the spark of a match—intense, thrilling, and full of promise. But with that spark comes vulnerability, the willingness to open oneself to another in both strength and fragility. This section explores the raw beauty of desire, the comfort and chaos of intimacy, and the quiet ache that lingers in the heart's deepest corners. These poems are a window into the moments when love consumes, transforms, and ultimately leaves its mark.

Made Before the Universe

Before time had a name, we were together –
Not as two, but as one,
A single mass cradled in the arms of the universe,
Waiting for the first breath of existence.
In that timeless expanse, we knew each other
Without words, without bodies,
Just particles woven so tightly,
No separation could be imagined.

But then the universe spoke,
And in that eruption of light and energy,
We were scattered –
Atoms torn from atoms,
Drifting through space and time,
Carried on the winds of creation.

Now, we float in different forms,
But the essence of you has always been with me,
Stardust in my blood,
Your presence lingering in the spaces
Between my breaths.
It's as if every cell in me remembers you,
Aching with a kind of quiet longing,
Reaching across the vastness of what was torn
apart.

And though we live in different skins,
Though the distance between us feels endless,

Love and Longing

I know, with a certainty that runs
Deeper than the stars,
That my particles were once fused to yours,
And they call to you still.

It's not just desire, not just want –
It's a pull, a need to be whole again.
For in you,
I see the reflection of all that I once was,
All that we once were.
And when I hold you, when I touch you,
It's not just skin against skin,
It's the universe remembering itself,
Finding the pieces it lost when the stars were
born.

And in that reunion, however brief,
The cosmos quiets,
And for a moment,
We are one again.

How I Crave Your Perfect Imperfections

You tell me you want to be perfect for me,
But my love for you was found in the spaces,
Between all you call imperfect,
In the contours of your insecurities
And the beauty that lives quietly within.

I love the profile you try to hide,
The hands you think too worn or plain,
The accent you tease yourself about,
As if it could make you anything less
Than beautiful.

My love rests in the places you overlook,
In the shadows cast by your flaws,
In those hidden angles and rough edges,
That you keep just out of reach,
Believing they need to be smoothed away.

You are already perfect to me,
Not in spite of these things,
But because of them.
Each quirk, each imperfection, each scar –
They are what make you whole,
A mosaic of beauty, raw and undeniable.

So, don't try to be flawless for me;
You've been more than enough
From the start.

Love and Longing

For it's in the details, you wish to erase
That I find the truest reflection
Of my love for you –
In the spaces between what you see
As imperfect,
You are perfect,
Exactly as you are.

Fingers Woven in Hair

My fingers weave firmly into your hair,
Each strand a tether pulling you closer,
As I tilt your head back, baring your throat,
The smooth expanse of skin
Laid open for me,
Soft and vulnerable, a quiet surrender.

My tongue traces its way along your neck,
Slow and deliberate, savoring each inch,
Leaving a trail of warmth
That rises to your cheeks,
Each flick of contact drawing out
That delicate whimper I've come to crave.

Your knees begin to falter,
Yet you hold still,
Trusting my hands to steady you,
A silent promise between us,
In the gentle strength of my grip
Firm but reverent,
Claiming but never cruel.

I pull you closer, feel your pulse
Quicken beneath my touch,
And your breath shivers out in anticipation,
As I bring my lips to your ear,
The warmth of my growled whisper,
A low command that settles into your bones —

"You're mine"

And with a soft, trembling exhale,
You answer,

"I'm yours,"

A declaration, not of submission alone,
But of trust deeper than words can reach,
A yielding only given in freedom,
In the safety we create,
Bound by choice.

Our love is woven in this dance,
In the tender strength of held wrists,
The gentle bruises of shared abandon,
Where the world fades, and its just us,
A rhythm of breaths and heartbeats,
Each touch a vow,
Each whisper a reminder –
That in this space, you are seen,
Cherished, adored,
In every raw, vulnerable, powerful part of you.

Green Eyed Monster of your Breathing

I'm jealous of the air
That kisses your skin, every hour, every day,
Slipping across you,
Touching your softness
I ache to feel beneath my hands.

I envy the sunlight,
The way it pours over you,
Warming every curve, tracing
The edges of you
That my fingers can only dream to know.

I'm jealous of the alcohol
You take readily inside,
The way it becomes part of you,
Filling spaces I can only reach
In fleeting moments.

I envy the music,
That pulls you under,
Where you close your eyes,
And disappear into its embrace,
Leaving me here, outside
Of that beautiful world.

I'm jealous of the thoughts
That live within your mind,
That brush against your heart

[14]

Love and Longing

In secret,
Keeping pieces of you hidden
From me

And I envy the blood
Held within your heart,
Pumping life through you
Beating close to your soul,
When all I want is to be there,
To live in that sacred,
Hidden place.

Overwhelming Pleasure of Authority

The room is dim, shadows casting shapes across
Your skin,
My fingers, just barely there, trace the line of
Your neck,
A slow, deliberate path,
As I feel the rise
Of each breath you take,
Your body soft, pliant, waiting,
Yet already surrendered,
I hover close, the heat between us thick,
My breath grazes your ear, warm, teasing,
And I feel the shiver that courses through you,
Not from cold, but from the unspoken promise,
Of what comes next.

Your skin hums beneath my touch,
Each stroke a command, each pause a test
Of your patience,
I explore you with deliberate care,
The curve of your waist,
The softness of your thigh,
My hands claiming without haste,
Yet you feel it,
The quiet authority in every movement.
You yield, instinctively, beautifully,
Your body arches,
Offering itself to the control I hold,
The air thickens, heavy with anticipation,

Love and Longing

Your pulse quickens under my fingers,
And I know you're lost in this space I create.

I press you back, firm but not rushed,
Your lips part in a quiet gasp,
A silent plea that I acknowledge
But do not yet answer.
Instead,
I let the moment stretch,
Drawing out the tension like a taut string,
Waiting to snap, but not yet.
Your wrists in my grasp, your breath shallow,
I can feel your surrender, the unspoken need,
For me to take what I will, as you fall deeper,
Into this dance of power and touch,
Where every caress binds you closer to my will,
And every pause makes you ache for more.

The silence between us is thick,
Broken only by your soft,
Barely contained moans,
And the quiet satisfaction I feel
As you give yourself,
Completely to the dominance of my touch.
Your skin, your breath, your need –
It all belongs to me now,
And with every move, I remind you,
That in this moment, I control the pleasure,
I decide when it begins,
And when it overwhelms you.

See Ya Later, 256

There it stands, hushed
In twilight,
Its walls peeled back, open to
The wind,
A frame caught between
The past and what's next.

Once, it held the quiet glances,
The soft laugh barely contained,
Moments stitched in shadows
And light.

Dust motes danced in the morning beams,
Whispers softened by the hum
Of work.
Here, where words lingered in
The air,
And something gentle took root,
Unseen yet certain.

Corners that knew the warmth
Of secrets,
Held breaths and a touch, just
Shy of too much,
The promise folded quietly
Between the hours.

Now, as it's laid bare,

Love and Longing

I think of that space as a keeper,
Of small things and
Hidden smiles,
Of feelings that bloomed like
Wildflowers in an unremarkable place.

It may vanish, taken piece by piece,
Yet its bones hold echoes,
And the memories, sweet and shy,
Linger in the hollowed-out air.

In those walls, there's still a part
Of us –
A soft, forgotten spark,
Flickering.

Submissive

In the space between command and surrender,
You wait – breath caught; eyes lowered –
Silent, yet begging in every curve of your body,
My hand hovers, a whisper before touch,
Control tightening around us both,
As my grip holds your slender throat,
And desire coils like smoke in the air.

You're beautiful when you kneel,
The world fading until there is only us –
A word, a breath, and you obey,
My name soft on your lips,
Yours held hostage between my teeth.

I pull you closer –
Skin to skin, gasp to gasp –
Your will is mine to shape,
But your pleasure, belongs to you.
And in this give and take, this push and pull,
We find the freedom that only surrender brings.

Forever Light

She is the unsetting sun,

Burning on the horizon

Refusing to let me sleep

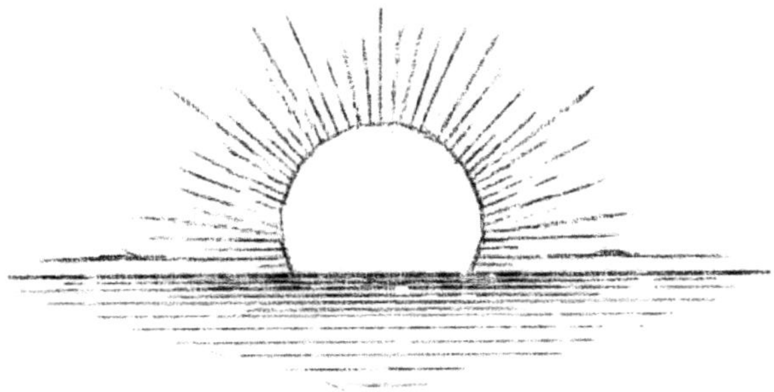

Throat

The look on your face,
Your eyes widen then close,
Rolling back,
Mouth opened,
Brow furrowed.
The silent moan,
And gasp of pleasure,
As my hand grips your throat,
The way your body pushes against mine,
In that moment,
Your desire to be controlled.
The soft whimper that escapes,
Between your soft inviting lips
Draws me closer to you.
The soft breath of my whisper,
Against your ear
"Good girl".

Parasitic Love

It landed softly, unseen, unheard,
Loves needle pierces deep, like a silent word.
A parasite, it burrows in my soul,
Rewriting my will, taking control.

I am no longer the one I was,
My mind is yours, and it's just because…
Like the wasp that lays its egg in me,
Your love hatches, and now I cease to be.

Fungi creeping through the bark of trees,
So does your love turn my thoughts to disease.
I move like a puppet, my strings pulled tight,
Every action for you, no longer my fight.

A hollow body, a host to your will,
I dance, I breathe, but my soul is still.
A zombie now, I serve your need,
No self remains, only love's planted seed.

You, the master, and I, the prey,
In loves parasitic grip, I decay.
Fed on until I am no more,
Love's hunger leaves me empty, sore.

Ropelessly Bound Together

I watch as you unfold beneath me,
A delicate petal softened by evening light,
Offering yourself in quiet surrender,
Your breath a whispered invitation,
Your skin a canvas warmed by desire,
Waiting for my touch to etch its claim.
Your gaze falls, shy but wanting,
The pulse at your throat a rhythm I command,
Each beat a silent vow,
Each breath a sigh beneath my hands, yielding to
The weight of my presence,
A tension drawn taut between what is
And what could be.
You arch, a tide rising to meet my pull,
hands open, palms bare as if to say,
Take me, I am yours,
And in that moment, you are mine—
Bound not by rope, but by trust,
The tender ache of giving,
Of being held,
Of knowing that every inch of you
Belongs to me.

My voice becomes the only sound you hear,
Its cadence a slow descent into darkness,
A silk thread pulling you deeper,
Until the world narrows to this space,

Love and Longing

This electric hum between us,
And you fall, unshielded,
Into the depths of my gaze,
Knowing I will catch you, lift you,
Shape you to the contours of my desire.

You yield to the strength of my hands,
To the silent promises traced along your skin,
The slow, measured weight
That brings you down,
Holds you steady,
Until you are liquid, molten,
Poured into my palms,
A whispered plea written
In the language of touch,
And l, unwavering,
Am the one who answers.

Love Cancer

It starts as a whisper, a shadowed mass,
Barely seen, barely felt, but growing fast.
A tumor forms in the chambers of the heart,
Loves first seed, the slow decay begins to start.

Cells divide, multiplying in their hold,
Roots stretching deep, a grip so cold.
It spreads like fire, veins tangled and tight,
Infiltrating the mind, turning day into night.

Love metastasizes, first to the brain,
Where thoughts of you become my pain,
In every corner, every fold, you dwell,
Turning thoughts to obsessions I cannot quell.

Now hollowed out, a shell remains,
Drained of self, but love sustains.
I am not me, but only you,
Love, the cancer, which devoured me through.

No longer whole, no longer free,
The tumor of love has consumed me.
In the marrow of my every bone you thrive,
Leaving just enough of me to stay alive.

Evolution of Love and Death

Wake, eat, sleep repeat
A rhythm steady, day complete.
Another sun, another moon,
Life unchanged, all too soon.

Then –
Wake, her, eat, sleep, repeat,
Her name a whisper, soft and sweet.
A thought at dawn, a thought at dusk,
Faint yet growing, like a rush.

Now –
Wake, her, eat, her, sleep, repeat,
The pull of her, more bittersweet.
Her taste, her scent, her voice so near,
She is a feast, she disappears.

Until –
Wake, her, her, sleep, she fades,
Life's routine begins to trade.
Her presence, loud, consumes my mind,
A heart beats out of sync, confined.

Soon –
Her, wake, her, sleep, no space to keep,
A cancerous love metastasized deep.
It spreads, it grows, no cure in sight,
Consumes the day, devours the night.

Finally –
Her, wake, her, no sleep at all,
In every thought and every call
She's every breath, my pulse, my fear,
Love entwined, she's all that's here.

The Impermanence of the Permanent

Her name still lies upon my chest,
Ink pressed deeper when I was just seventeen,
An age when love seemed like forever
And permanence was found in the needle's sting.
But the years have worn the lines,
And though the letters remain on my skin,
They are no longer carved into my heart.

What was once a mark of devotion,
A seal of youthful, reckless love,
Has faded into something softer –
The echo of a promise made by a boy
Who thought they'd never change.

Childhood sweethearts grew into friends,
The ink now merely a shadow of a past we shared,
While loves true flame finds its home elsewhere.
For her name rest on my chest,
Another is stamped within my heart,
A love unspoken in ink yet indelible,
Deep in places no needle could reach.

Its she who owns each beat,
Her name etched not in ink, but in pulse,
An unmarked truth, unwavering and raw,
A love that's bound not by needles or skin,
But by something no tattoo could ever hold.

Section 2: Heartbreak and Loss

When love ends, it doesn't disappear—it leaves echoes, a lingering pulse that haunts the spaces left behind. Heartbreak is both a wound and a scar, a reminder of what was and what will never be. In this section, we step into the aftermath of love lost: the emptiness, the anger, the regret. These words capture the painful beauty of loss, the way it carves itself into memory and reshapes the soul.

Needless Needleless Compass

I am a compass stripped of its needle,
Lost in an endless night,
Spinning with no direction,
No purpose in the pull of this earth.
What is breath but hollow air,
A cruel mimic of life,
When the rhythm of my heart
Can no longer beat to the sound of her?

The sky falls heavy,
A weight pressing down on my chest,
And every second without her is a scream
Echoing through the silence.
What is time but a slow suffocation,
A countdown to oblivion
When the only pulse that matters
Is hers, and it is gone from me?

I am a body with no blood
Heart with no song,
A flame with no heat.
I wander untethered,
Through the dark,
And without her,
There is no morning,
No horizon,
No point to the next step,
The next breath.

Home(less) is where the Heart is(n't)

When we kiss,
Theres a warmth in my chest,
A fire that starts low,
Spreading through my bones,
A kind of comfort
Only you could ignite.

When I miss you,
It's an ache that digs deep,
Something heavy that won't leave,
It pulls at my chest,
Takes the breath right out of me.
I keep hoping the days will be kinder,
But they're hollow without you,
Like an echo in an empty room.

When I drink
It's a burning –
Maybe it helps for a while,
Maybe it numbs the sharp edges,
But the flame can't replace
The way it feels
To hold you in my arms,
When everything finally makes sense.
The world stops spinning,
I stop running,
And I know what it means,
To be home.

Heartbreak and Loss

Without you,
There's a void,
A black hole in my chest,
Taking pieces of me,
Bit by bit.
I'm half alive,
Half here, half gone,
Waiting for the moment
You fill that space again,
So I can finally live fully,
Without the emptiness that's left.
When you aren't beside me.

Rosary Beads of Broken Dreams

Despite everything—
The bruises beneath my skin that only I can feel,
The hollow ache that settles
Like winter in my chest,
The nights spent staring into darkness,
Counting memories
Like broken beads slipping through my fingers—
I still find her name etched
In the marrow of my bones.
Each letter carved deep,
A silent vow I can't unmake,
No matter how many times I bleed trying.

She is there,
Woven into the rhythm of my pulse,
An ache that refuses to leave,
The weight pressing against my ribs,
Soft and relentless,
Like the ocean gnawing at stone,
Wearing me down, bit by bit,
Until I am shaped by the force of her absence,
Sculpted by the space she left behind.

I've tried to bury it,
To dig down deep and hide it
In the corners of my mind,
But love, real love, is stubborn, unyielding,

Heartbreak and Loss

A seed that grows even in the darkest soil,
Roots tangling around memories,
Binding me to her,
So tightly I fear I'll lose myself
If I try to pull them free.

Sometimes I wonder if this is what it means
To be alive and hurting,
To feel the sharp edges of love cutting
Deeper than any wound I could trace with my
Own hands.
Because even in the wreckage,
In the ruin of what we were,
I am helpless to do anything but love her still,
Helpless against the quiet truth of it,
Like breath, like blood, like gravity,
An ache that is both prison and peace,
Both hurt and home.

I know no end to this,
No horizon where she does not wait for me,
Even as she fades from my grasp,
Even as her shadow pulls away.
And maybe,
That is the cost of a heart that loves deeply—
To carry the weight of her in every step I take,
To be haunted by the beauty and the pain
Of what was,
And of what will always be.

Forgotten Flame

I was fire once,
Burning bright in your gaze,
But now my heat spreads like poison,
Slow, crawling, suffocating.
It starts in the chest-
A flicker that won't fade-
Then spirals through my veins,
Barbed wire wrapped around blood,
Tightening, tearing,
Reminding me I was never enough.

The silence weighs heavy,
Heavier than words ever did.
I believed – God, I believed –
That I was more than just a shadow
Fading in your light.
But now, each heartbeat mocks me,
Whispers of stupidity,
Echoes of promises
That never belonged to me.

I am forgotten,
Left to crumble beneath the weight
Of all the things I thought I was.
And still, the heat burns,
Searing through me,
A cruel reminder
That I once held something
That never existed.

Silent Lips

As my name
Falls silent on your
Lips
Yours forever
Echoes in my heart

Playlist of Pain

Our playlist still plays.
I still drink,
But you're not here.
Particles of us drift apart,
No longer do I dance.
Or smile.
I wanna be yours,
But all I do is sit,
Face down
Crying over what's *broken.*

Six billion voices around me,
Yet I only miss yours.
Drawing pins line the path of memories,
Sharp, unavoidable.
I *just pretend* I'm fine,
But it's all a lie.

I miss your touch,
The sound of your laughter,
The way we'd wrap around each other,
Undisclosed desires, burning between us.
Birds of a feather,
We moved through the music –
Smiling,
Kissing,
Like we were lost in *Amsterdam*

But you're not here.
I'm alone,
Staring at *the red* of another empty evening,
Broken.

The Whispered Lies from Empty Bottles

Resisting the urge to reach out
I pull my poison from the shelf.
Hard to count the minutes I miss you,
When drowning in the bottom of a bottle.

I trace your name on the glass,
Lips sealed, afraid you'd hear
The echo of my shame.
Each minute hangs heavy,
A weight I carry through another drink,
But time won't numb this ache.

The bottle whispers lies –
"I'm easier to hold than the silence she left."
I let it speak for me,
Each sip a word unsaid,
Each drop a memory erased.

Your voice, a distant lullaby,
Can't quiet this storm anymore.
What once felt warm now cuts like ice.
The comfort of you slipping further away.

I wrestle with the need to call,
But pride chains me down,
And I sip the night away,
Waiting for the courage
To reach beyond the bottle,
To where you once were.

Shame

What a shame
That I miss us enough
For us both

Self-Immolation

Fire within my shell,
Burning my ink-stained skin
Is this anger, or the final breath of hope
Embarrassment? Or realization
That you never truly cared?

Flames rise, cauterizing my nerves,
Sealing the pathways of feeling,
Each spark a memory that won't fade,
Yet I scorch them all away,
Letting ash replace the scars of touch.

I burn so I may never burn again,
A blaze set by my own hand,
To keep your coldness from seeping in.
No tears, no pleas, no cracks in this armor,
For I have set fire to what was once soft.

Now, the embers dim inside me,
Smoke curls where love used to breathe,
This is the price of caring too much –
I turn to ash, untouched by pain,
Never to feel, never to hope again.

Broken Hearted Silence

I used to wonder
What the sound of a broken heart might be –
Shattered glass?
Splintered paving stones?
Or the soft tear of flesh?
I wonder no longer.

For the silence of a broken heart
Is nothing.

Nothing compared to the wreckage of happiness,
To the animal howl,
The primal scream
Of love,
Lost.

The Noose at the end of the Hope

The smallest part of my mind
That guards the last untouched piece of my heart
The thinnest sliver, not yet devoured
By this love for you,
Cries out – pleads for me to walk away.

But the ache of this love
Has woven itself into my bones.
I no longer know who I am without it.
How else could I fill my days
If not with dreams of you?
What purpose does time hold,
If not spent thinking of you?

What is life without hope?
To walk away would be to murder hope –
And so, to save my life,
I will die a little more each day,
Waiting.
Hoping.
For the love
That will never come

Whiplash

The sound of glass cascading upon the ground
Crumpled metal body work
Sudden stop
But my momentum keeps me going
The whiplash from your mood
Your words
Inconsistent
Encouraging acceleration
Into the brick wall
Damaged and broken
What use is there in repairing myself
When the same wall awaits me
As moods change
And you need a ride
Again.

The Carousel of Silence

The silence wraps me like a noose,
Each day a bruise, unseen but heavy,
Her absence, a knife that cuts
With precision
And I wear it like a second skin

I pour tequila into the ache,
NyQuil follows, a bitter lullaby,
Wishing to fade into blackness,
Because even the air tastes like goodbye.

I want to carve her name in my bones,
Feel it like a pulse, a scream,
But the blade is dull,
And the scream is swallowed by
The empty room.

Seven days stretch like lifetimes,
Each one heavier than the last,
And my hands shake,
Not from the cold,
But from the weight of not knowing
If I still exist in her mind.

Then –
A message, a flicker, a breath of her,
The screen lights up and I drown in it,
Suddenly the tequila burns less,

Heartbreak and Loss

The air grows soft like a sigh,
And the sun spills warmth across my skin
Like she's here, like she remembers.

But the silence waits,
A shadow at my back,
And I know it will come again,
And I will drink, I will bleed,
Until her voice turns the tide
Once more.

Turn off the Moonlight

I am the moon,
Silent, pale, suspended in a sky too vast,
A surface of craters and cold stone,
Trapped in orbit around the one thing
That gives me light

You are the sun,
Uncontainable, fierce in your burn,
Casting warmth across my pocked terrain,
Filling my emptiness with your glow.

Without you,
I am left in shadows,
My light only a memory,
Fading as I drift in darkness,
A hollow rock in the vast still night.

For I am nothing but reflection,
A silent echo of your fire,
Lost without your blaze to hold me,
A quiet, empty thing,
Waiting only for your return.

What did I do Wrong?

I remember how your words used to arrive –
Quick and full, like the surge of an
Incoming tide,
Each message an invitation,
A pulse that drew me into your
World.

I could hear the warmth in you
Laughter,
See it spilling through the spaces
Between our texts,
Words breathing, electric with
Something unspoken.
You didn't need to say it; I felt it
Like sunlight breaking through.

But now, it's as if the air has thinned,
Like stars fading one by one
In the quiet of dawn.
Our exchanges fall into the hollow
Of long pauses,
And your words have become
Fragments,
One-word answers that barely echo.

I used to wait for your messages,
Knowing they would feel alive,
Charged with a feeling we never had to name.

Heartbreak and Loss

Now I wait for the absence,
For the silence that has learned to fill
The space where you once were.

You are still there, but distant,
A shadow moving behind a closed door.
I went from being a light in your eyes,
To a flicker, to a memory,
Until I became no one,
Lost somewhere between
What was and what could have been.

Cradle of Silence

To be nothing
To the one who is everything
Is to feel the weight of emptiness –
A heart held out,
Cradling only silence.

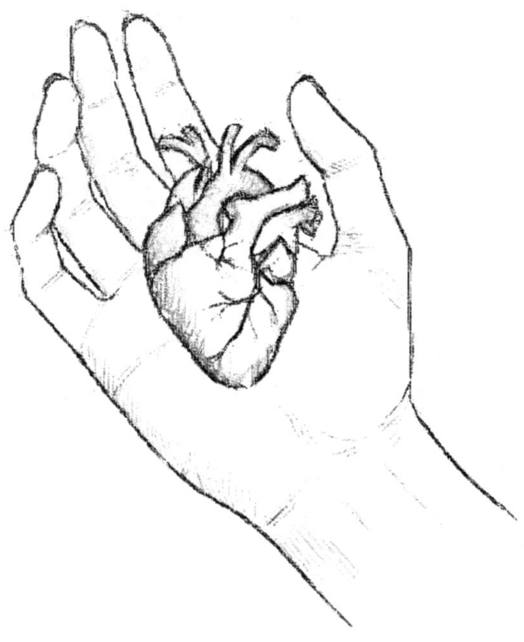

Eric Wimp is….. Bananaman

You peeled away my skin,
Worthless, damaged, stripped bare,
Discarded to rot and crumble into the ground,
Its only use now to feed you,
To enrich the soil beneath your feet,
Nourishing the beauty you wear so effortlessly,
While I fade, an offering you devour
With teeth bared and eager.

My insides are yours, hollowed out,
Devoted and consumed,
Each bite you take carving deeper,
Hungrily, greedily, without pause,
Teeth marks etched in the softest places,
Leaving nothing untouched,
No part of me unscarred.

And when I am nothing,
When you've taken all there is,
I will disappear without echo,
No more than a fleeting stain in the earth,
A memory turned to dust,
Just another you decimated,
Swallowed and forgotten,
While you flourish, unmarked,
My absence feeding your roots,
My ruin nourishing your bloom.

Why?

Why did you do this to me
Make me fall in love with you
Let me go deep down the well
Landing in a shallow puddle of stagnant water
Light unable to reach me
Fingernails lost to the mortar of the walls
Desperate to claw back to your warmth
As you slide the lid
Over my source of air
To suffocate in my need for you.

Reversing the Poles

We were two magnets,
Spinning in a silent pull,
Invisible threads binding us,
Tethered tight and trembling,
As if the universe itself could not
Keep us apart.

But something shifted,
A quiet reversal, unseen,
Like dusk bleeding into night,
And I felt the hum inside you
Dull,
The weight of your pull slipping,
Leaving my hands empty, aching,
Like reaching for a hand that
Vanishes at dawn.

Now, you're here,
But your presence is a cold deflection,
A current that pushes me away,
As if the charge we shared
Has twisted into something strange,
Something foreign.

I am still drawn
To the memory of you,
To the ghost of that gravity
We once shared,

Heartbreak and Loss

But each step pulls me
Deeper into the hollow space
Where your warmth once sparked.

I stand here, longing for that pull,
And you stand there,
Silent,
No longer the force I knew,
But a shadow of it,
A flicker in the vast and
Aching dark.

If I Sleep Forever, Will you Always be There?

I close my eyes,
I see you stood in white,
My eyes turn to oceans,
Knowing when they open,
You'll be gone.

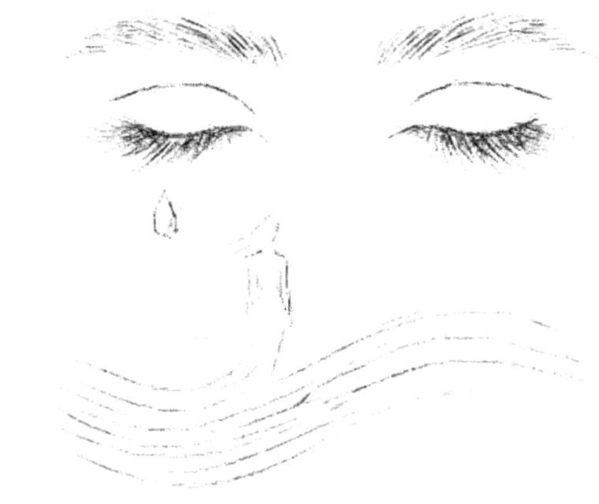

Cruelty of a Broken Heart that Still Beats

The cruelest thing about a broken heart
Is that it betrays you,
Pumping life into limbs that ache to let go,
Pulling breath into lungs that don't want to hold it,
Keeping you here, anchored,
In a world that feels like a stranger's shadow.

It still works,
It still beats, steady as a lie,
Each pulse mocking the hollow ache,
Each thud a reminder of everything that's gone
And everything that stays
When you wish it wouldn't.

A heart like this –
It doesn't know mercy.
It doesn't know how to stop
The memories from rising like tides,
The vision of what was,
What could have been,
What will never be.

And so, it feels, stubborn and relentless,
Bearing the weight of what you cannot forget,
Refusing to surrender, to numb, to fall silent.
It keeps you alive in the cruelest way,
Carrying on, heartbeat by forsaken heartbeat,
When all you want is peace.

Entangled Within the Universe Indifference

There is no cure for this—
No pill or prayer or passage of time,
Just the relentless pulse of you
In every quiet space,
In every night that fades to morning
Without you beside me.

My heart is bound,
Caught in the fabric of something unseen,
Strung across an impossible distance,
Threaded through shadows and starlight,
Where I am pulled to you, always,
Like a river drawn to the ocean
Without question or hesitation.

I am entangled—
Not just connected,
But fused at the smallest, silent particle,
A spark in my chest that mirrors yours,
No matter how far you drift.
And so, I can't love another;
Their hands would feel like lies,
Their breath a foreign wind.

With you, I am whole,
A whisper against the universe's indifference,
But without you,
I am left in the hollows between heartbeats,

Heartbreak and Loss

Waiting for something that may never come,
Anchored to a promise
You never made but that my soul remembers.

I exist in this suspended state—
Forever on the edge of joy or despair,
The weight of both crushing me slowly.
For there is no in-between,
No escape from the sharpness of knowing
That I am yours
Or I am nothing at all.

So, I will stand here, alone,
In the ache of this truth,
My heart a compass spinning,
Locked to you,
In love or in loss,
Forever bound,
Forever waiting

Once, the Dark feared our Flames

We were fire in the dark,
Two flames flickering close enough to touch,
Close enough to feel the heat of one another,
But never allowed to merge,
Kept apart by the thin, invisible lines
Drawn by time,
Or fate, or some ancient hand
That whispered no.

In you, I found the pulse I'd been missing,
A rhythm that sang through my bones,
An ache that settled soft in my chest,
Both pleasure and pain,
A bruise I pressed just to feel alive.

We held each other
As if the night was ours alone,
As if dawn would never come to steal us back,
Our breaths mingling, weaving invisible threads,
Binding us in a way the world could not see,
A language spoken only in touch,
In glances,
In the quiet space between words.
And yet, we are kept apart,
Two halves of a song
Caught on different winds,
Echoing through the same silence,

Heartbreak and Loss

Calling to one another,
Knowing the answer
Will never reach us.

Still, I carry you —
Your touch like a secret
Folded into my skin,
Your voice an echo I hold in my mouth,
Swallowed down
When the longing grows too sharp,
When the distance becomes a fire
That only memories can douse.
We are here,
In separate worlds, still burning,
Still reaching,
Two hearts lit
From the same flame,
Forever in orbit,
Close but never close enough
To burn as one.

Solo Reflection in a Lake of Tears

How do I let you go
When every breath scrapes your name
Across my lungs,
And closing my eyes only brings you closer,
Etched into the darkness behind my lids?

Every thought is a return,
A relentless loop that spirals back to you.
The ache is unyielding, raw,
An open wound I can't help but press.

There is no numbness here,
Only a pain that burrows deeper,
An ache that swells with each beat.
Tears blur my vision but sharpen your
Absence,
And pool at my feet,
And in their surface, I see myself –
Untethered,
Drifting,
Stripped bare in a world without you.

Little Water

I can't drink vodka anymore,
I'll never taste like it did
When I drew it off her lips
Sweet as stolen sin.

What used to warm, now sears —
A slow burn that scars,
Scorching away the remnants
Of what we were.

It douses the fire we kindled,
Only to ignite something darker,
An ache that smolders in
The hollow places,
Spreading through my veins,
A wildfire fed by memories
I can't seem to drown

The Sadistic Sommelier

They brought you to me
Like a glass, dark with promise,
Set it down, let me linger on the scent,
That first taste blooming across my tongue
In whispers of memories and all that might be.

I breathed you in, felt the richness,
Notes of something deeper –
As if aged just for me.
And I thought, yes, this is the one.

But then, before I could claim it,
Before the warmth could settle,
The glass was pulled away,
The bottle wrapped tight, hidden,
Carried to some place I could never reach.

Now I sit here, glass empty,
Staring at the stain of you,
Left upon my lips, aching for more,
While the memory of that taste
Burns down to silence,
Leaving me with the shadow
Of something almost mine.

What it is to be poured a life in a glass
Only to sip, savor, and know
That even the smallest taste
Can leave you thirsting for a lifetime?

(Life)Time Bomb

You planted a bomb in me,
One I cannot diffuse,
I've traced every wire,
But I stop short each time,
Almost hoping not to find the right one.

I've fumbled with the cutters,
Half-hearted in my attempts,
Drawn to the thrill of its ticking.
Each beat an echo of something deeper,
A dangerous melody that I cant bear to silence.

Theres no timer I can see,
No countdown I could reset,
Only the quiet promise that someday,
When this bomb finally erupts,
It will be the final symphony of my heart.

I carry it willingly,
Each scar a vow carved in flesh,
Knowing that to sever these wires
Would be to lose the love I cradle close.

So, I live with this silent fuse,
A life intertwined with its burn,
Accepting that this bomb you left
Will hold my heart until my dying breath.

Pause

Theres a quiet pause,
A delay of peace when I open my eyes
Each morning, and it hasn't yet hit me
That you're gone.
Its reminiscent of the way
A blade kisses my skin,
All seeming well, just for a moment,
Until the blood rises slowly to the surface,
A truth I can no longer ignore.

Both leave scars I'll never recover from.

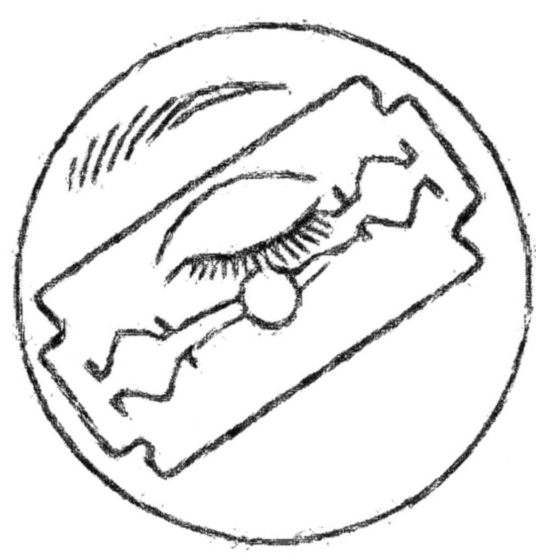

Drowning in an Ocean of Magnetic Tides

I am caught in the pull of a magnetic tide,
Drawn to you,
Helpless against the swell.
Every time I reach the shore,
You slip back,
A wave retreating into itself,
Leaving me stranded,
Soaked in want,
The salt of longing drying to my skin.

When I pull away,
Try to drift to calmer waters,
You surge forward,
A tide that refuses to release me,
Calling me back
With a force as invisible
As it is relentless,
Magnetic.

Buit when I turn to you,
Aching for closeness,
You reced,
Slipping from my grasp,
An undertow I cant hold,
Pulling me under.
I gasp for air in the riptide of this want,
Waves crashing over me,
Relentless,

Barely letting me breathe before the next pull,
Drags me down.

At this point,
I welcome drowning,
The darkness that follows surrender,
For at least then I'll take you deep within me,
Holding you as I'm finally embraced by peace.
After the first sting of salt,
The burn of lungs,
I will drift, fading into the depths,
Washed out into silence,
Where the waves no longer rise,
And you can no longer pull away.

Don't Let us Be Just Smoke

If I get over you,
If the wounds you carved in my heart
Begin to close,
Scar over,
Thick and pale,
Will it mean that all of this,
Was just a passing storm,
A bruise that fades with time,
Leaving only faint traces
Of the ache that once consumed me?

If I can breathe without feeling you,
If my nights no longer echo
With the ghost of your voice,
Will it mean that everything we were,
Every whispered promise,
Ever soft touch,
Was nothing more than fleeting smoke,
Lost in the air,
Vanishing like you did?

If I let you go,
If I learn to forget,
Will the love I held so fiercely
Have been just another story,
A page that turns,
Leaving me wondering
If it was real at all?

A Ribcage of Wax and Smoke

You are the wick threaded deep
Within my heart of wax,
The one who struck the match
And set me aflame.
I burn because of you,
Melt and drip,
Molten rivulets tracing paths
Down my ribs,
Each drop a heave bead
Pooling within,
Solidifying into hardened scars,
Layer upon layer,
Sealing memories inside me.

Your breath feeds my flame,
A whisper of oxygen
Just enough to make me glow,
Just enough to keep me alive
In your warmth –
Until you turn away,
And the air thins,
Leaving me spluttering,
Grasping at remnants of the spark,
You kindled with careless hands.

I feel myself spilling over,
Puddles of desire and despair,

Cooling,
Clinging to the edges of my chest.
Still, I burn on,
A slow candle dying,
Spitting embers, sparking in desperation,
While you draw nearer
Only to pull away,
Leaving me hollowed out,
Half formed,
A hollow sculpture
Shaped by your heat.

In the end,
I know you will snuff me out —
Thumb pressed to the wick,
Pinching the flame with the same hand,
That once lit me alive.
And I will be left,
Frozen in place, a heart of wax,
Hardened and cracked,
Forever bearing the shape
Of your touch.

My Love was Clay, Poured into Your Mold, Baked in a Misguided Kiln of Hope

The stillness within me,
A silence so thick it swallows the room,
As if even the air held its breath
When you walked away.
Blood gathers heavy in my feet,
Rooting me to a floor that feels foreign,
Each step forward pulling me deeper
Into a space where memory frays,
Where all sense of self slips from my hands,
Disappearing like shadows at dawn.

I had given so much,
Poured every piece of love I held
Into the shape of you,
A devotion carved into bone,
Written into the rhythm of my pulse.
But as you turned,
As your presence faded to a memory,
I felt myself unravel,
A man losing his own reflection,
Becoming anonymous to himself.,

What am I now
But an echo of love left behind?
A question without answer,
A name I no longer recognize.

Who was I
before you filled my empty spaces?
And now,
As I stand hollowed and still,
Will I exist once you're gone,
Or was I only every real
In the moments I loved you?

Shards in Shaking Bloody Hands

Though my heart lies in pieces,
Shattered by your leaving,
I find myself on hands and knees,
Searching through the dark for every shard,
As if gathering fragments
Of a once- whole sky,
Each piece a constellation of memories,
Each one sharp with the weight of you.

I could leave them here, scattered,
Let dust and time bury their jagged edges,
But I can't bear the thought of a heart
Without the ache of your absence,
Or hands empty of the work
Of piecing together what once held you.

So I spend my days in devotion,
Fingers bleeding as I fit the fragments,
Rebuilding every crack, every scar,
In hopes they'll form something
You might hold again.
With each piece that slips,
Each cut that opens,
I know its futile – and yet, I go on,
Knowing that the pain itself binds me to you.

I'll keep this heart
Fragile and flawed,

Heartbreak and Loss

A stained-glass window of longing,
Its fractures softened by the light
Of memories,
Each one a promise
I made to myself,
To love you with all the pieces I have,
Even if you return
Just to break them again.

And when I close my eyes each night,
I feel the weight of that heart,
Heavy yet alive,
A monument to love and loss,
Held together not by hope,
But by a raw, relentless faith
That someday, these hands
Trembling, scarred, and bloody,
Might lay this heart at your feet,
Whole enough for you to recognize,
And, perhaps, gentle enough
for you to keep.

The Uncaged Bird with Stockholm Syndrome

You are the cage,
And I am the bird who once nestled within,
Now "free" but aching to return,
To press myself back
Against the bars of your heart.
When you opened the door,
You sealed it shut behind me,
Never once asking if I wanted to fly.

I was content with clipped wings,
Safe within the boundaries of you,
My feathers brushing against your chest,
The gentle flutter that once stirred you.

Now my wings are unwelcome,
A breeze that disrupts, unsettles,
And you, once my shelter,
Have become the cold wind
That drives me away.

You opened your cage to me once,
Let me rest against the beat of your heart,
And now, alone in the vastness of sky,
I am tossed against winds I can't fight,
With nowhere to land.
So, I'll keep beating these wings,
Fighting for something lost,

Until exhaustion drains me empty,
And I fall, lifeless, to the earth.
I will lie there, unrecognizable,
My body given back to the soil,
Consumed by insects,
Forgotten beneath an endless sky,
No longer the bird
Who once knew your love.

Short and Shattered

Though my heart lies in pieces,
Shattered by your leaving,
I will spend forever gathering each shard,
Piecing them back together,
Just for one more chance
To let you break it all over again.

Kafka's Apple for a Heart, Rotten to the Core

There is a place inside me,
Where love once thrived, red and ripe –
A heart that pulsed with life and hunger.
But now, it sits beneath my ribs,
A rotten apple,
Its flesh turned black, bitter with rejections.

I feel it decay, softening, sagging,
A bruise spreading through every vein,
Tender and unsightly, hidden from sight
Yet undeniable – a rot that festers within.

I want to carve it out,
To rid myself of the stench it brings,
But the body has grown over it,
An ugly wound I can't reach
Can't heal.
The skin around it tightens,
Holding this ruinous core in place,
Trapping me with something I can't release,
As if my bones are afraid to be empty.

Other sense it too –
Turning away, recoiling from the faintest whiff
Of something spoiled,
Something unworthy.
Their eyes glance, but never linger,
As though my hearts corruption

Seeps through,
Too vile to bear witness,
Too dark to approach.

I can't look at it either,
This heart,
Can't love it any more than they can.
It's not mine,
Not the way it once was.
This thing – this rotten core within –
Has made itself an intruder,
A parasite I carry,
Unwilling.

And every day, the rot spreads,
Swelling, festering,
Pushing against the walls
That hold it back,
A constant ache,
A reminder of something list,
Turned sour, turned vile,
As if love, once tasted,
Left nothing
But poison in its place.

A Scale of Destruction

The balance of the universe –
The more I love you,
The more I hate myself
For doing so.

You've become my new addiction,
My newest form of self-mutilation,
Burning my insides like cheap whiskey,
Rattling through my mind like back-alley pills,
Carving my skin with blood-stained,
dollar store razor blades.

I suffer inwardly for you,
Aching in a hollow, endless agony,
Clinging to what was never to be.
Misguided hope nurtures the hatred
For myself.

The only happiness now
Lies in wishing for yours,
A small, bitter relief –
A sacrifice I've come to know.

(Re)Mixed Messages

I made a playlist of every song you sent,
A melody threaded with lies,
Each lyric a cruel untruth,
Echoing the promises that faded.

Each bass note cancels my heartbeat,
Each drop of sound a hollow thud,
And I die, moment by moment,
Wishing they were still ours,
That you still meant them.

But as I turn down the volume,
Another song arrives, unexpected,
Teasing with the flicker of tormenting hope.
You had me already, held me close,
So why twist the knife with remixed words,
Haunting me with verses once so real?

Every line a taunt, a whisper of might-have-been,
A reminder that you could have stayed –
Instead, you leave me drowning in songs
That feel like promises yet taste like ghosts.

While Your Cup Runneth over, Mine Runneth Dry

As I lay in the gutter,
Broken, bloody, dehydrated,
I reach out my hand to you,
Offering the last of my water.

You take it without pause,
Adding it to your overflowing cup,
While I fade beneath you,
Parched, unseen, and emptied.

Ritualistic Cigarettes and Alcohol

My lips ache, still shaped to your memory –
The tender touch, the hungry groan,
The way you left them bruised and softened,
Wet with words we never spoke.

Now they're met by the stale kiss
Of a cigarette,
Each drag a ghost of you,
Each exhale curling bitterly into the night.
Or I press the glass rim,
Whiskey sliding down,
Coating my throat,
Settling in my chest,
A slow burn that fails to warm,
The hollow spaces.

You've left me here,
Tracing your absence in small rituals –
The bite of smoke, the liquid fire,
The substitute touch,
A poor mimic of the real thing.
And in the silence,
I keep reliving the way
My lips fit to yours,
The way they still long to be held,
Like a secret too dangerous to name.

Section 3: Addiction and Numbness

There are moments when pain demands silence, a numbness that soothes like a cold compress on a burning wound. Addiction fills that void, offering comfort at a cost. This section explores the delicate line between solace and destruction, between seeking refuge and surrendering to dependency. In these poems, addiction becomes a companion, sometimes seductive, sometimes cruel, but always there, tempting one to escape from the world—and from oneself.

Clean

I miss you,
The way you made me feel –
Numbed all pain,
Medicated smiles,
Warmth spreading like fire through veins.

Then you leave,
And I ache for more.
Dependent on your touch,
Searching high and low
For something – anything –
To replace what you give.

I need you,
But I shouldn't.
You slowly kill me,
But I crave the numbness you bring,
The floating feeling,
Lost in the haze.
Of this opiate embrace –
Relief,
From pain,
From life.

Cocktail of Natural Sleep Aids

It starts the same way each night –
The familiar lineup set before me,
Antidepressant, whiskey, NyQuil,
A haze of tobacco smoke curling
Like a lullaby.
This bitter concoction is as normal to me
As coffee and cream are to the early risers
The only way sleep dares to find me now

I've lost count of the nights
When I drift off with a bottle in one hand
A blade in the other,
Steel biting into skin
As sharp as the burns in my throat
The bedsheets tell the story
In stains, splotches of spilled liquor
And streaks of crimson like dark.
Hidden confessions.
Sleep arrives in jagged
Breaths and half-dreams,
My body a weary canvas
Marked by the ritual,
A map of pain I trace in the dark,
Where only this cocktail
Knows my name
And whispers me to sleep.

Alcohol and Razor Blades

There's a bottle by the bed,
Half drained,
A friend that never questions.
It slips down easy,
Numbing the weight of all these tombstones
Piling on my chest.
I tip it back and swallow death,
One swig at a time.

Razor blades whisper
In the stillness of the night.
Their edge kisses my skin,
Delicate as the lies I tell myself.
Maybe it's the only way
To carve out some feeling
In this dead landscape
That used to be a heart.

Grief hangs heavy,
A fog I can't crawl out from under.
Every face I loved has turned to dust,
And I'm still here,
Breathing,
Aching,
Empty.
I cut just to feel something
In a world gone numb.
They tell me it gets better,

Addiction and Numbness

But they're not drowning
In the silence of rooms too quiet,
Or the scream of memories that won't fade.
They don't hold this bottle
Like a lifeline
Or drag this blade through skin
Like its some kind of salvation.

I'm alone,
With alcohol and razor blades.
They're the only ones who stay.

An Oasis of Hope within the Desert of Dependency

As I stumble through the unrelenting heat,
The dry discomfort of this arid desert of life,
My eyes fix on the horizon –
A shimmering oasis, a glint of relief,
Just out of reach. I ache to arrive,
To feel the cool rush of promised waters,
Each step a heavy pull forward,
A lurch into hope.
Every stumble tears my knees raw,
Burning on sand hot enough to form glass.

The ground beneath me is littered
With splinters of broken promises,
Shards of every empty bottle
That never lived up to its claim.

A taste of peace, but always fleeting –
Hope offered, then misery delivered,
Leaving lips cracked and throat parched,
Yearning, thirsting for one more drop.

Dependency wraps itself around me,
Thick as the haze of my own breath,
The lie so tempting I repeat it:
Just one more step, just one more drink,
And I'll reach it.

Jack and NyQuil fit the Bill, Never Diluted with Water

Two shot glasses
Lined up like old friends,
One for the edge, one for the guilt.
I pour Jack like it's medicine,
Watch the amber seep and sit, thick as memory,
My reflection broken across the glass.

It goes down slow, burns a little
Too much —
My throat a one-lane road to nowhere,
NyQuil close at hand,
Like some twisted promise
To knock me out clean,
Quiet the noise scraping at my skull.

I know I'll regret it,
The familiar sting of shame
The way morning will hit like judgement
With its indifferent light.
But right now, just let it be still,
Just let the room fade soft and dark.

I'm tired of holding my own bones together,
Tired of keeping my face
Straight and my hands
Steady,
While the pieces rattle underneath,

Loose and ugly.

Tonight, let the sleep
Take me down deep,
Past the regrets I keep
Close,
Past the emptiness I try to fill.
Tonight, let me drift
Into the hollow places,
No questions, no faces,
Just a little Jack,
A little green NyQuil,
And silence.

Section 4: Self-Harm and Self-Worth

Sometimes, the pain within becomes too much to contain, and it spills over, seeking release. Self-harm is a language of suffering, a manifestation of wounds too deep for words. These poems delve into the complex relationship with one's own body and mind, the struggle to cope with inner demons, and the desperate need to feel something—even if it's only pain. Here lies the rawest portrayal of self-conflict, where flesh meets sorrow.

The Needles of Life on the Vinyl of my Skin

The vinyl spins,
Its surface dark and glossy,
A deep black mirror
That holds my reflection,
In shards.
The needle drops,
A sharp edge pressing into the groove,
Its descent slow,
A dance of precision
And pain,
Tracing lines that seem endless,
Every crackle an ache,
Every pop a memory resurfacing.

The needle moves,
Weighted by the gravity of hurt,
Dragged along paths etched deep,
Into soft surface,
Each line,
Each groove a scar on the records skin,
Worn from play, replay,
The repetition of wounds reopened.

Some nights
I lift the needle myself,
Guiding it down with silent hands,
Letting it find familiar tracks,
Sinking into paths of least resistance,

Self-Harm and Self-Worth

Echoes of sounds only I can hear,
Softly repeating,
Like whispers carved in wax.

The vinyl hums,
Filling the quiet,
A song both broken
And whole,
A score written in spirals,
Held within grooves
That turn forever.

Each spin a question,
A moment traced in sound,
And I wonder if one day
I'll lift the needle gently,
Let it rest,
Leave the music unwound,
Find silence in a record,
No longer spinning.

Unbreakable Shadows in Fractured Mirrors

I stand before the glass,
And the reflection stares back,
A stranger carved from my own flesh,
A face I barely recognize,
Lined with regret, weighted with shame,
Bearing the spoils of my father's mistakes,
His cruelty etched into every line,
Scars that are not only mine but inherited,
Passed down like an unwanted heirloom.

I search the eyes that mirror mine,
Hoping for some glint of humanity,
Something that forgives, that understands,
But all I see is disdain,
A sneer twisted into every curve,
Mocking the skin I cannot shed,
Reminding me that his sins are my own,
That I carry his shadow under my skin.

This body-this brittle shell –
Holds nothing but ugliness.
The scars are carved confessions,
Written in a language of self-loathing,
A testament to the wars I wage within,
The battles I lose every night,
When the silence grows thick,
And I am left alone with this face,
This hated, hollow vessel.

Self-Harm and Self-Worth

I press fingers to flesh,
And feel nothing but disgust,
A twisted map of every failure,
Every broken promise
Scrawled across my skin,
As if I am nothing more
Than the sum of every scar,
Every bruise and every flaw,
Etched deeper with each glance.

I blame the person staring back,
For the weight I carry,
For the emptiness that gnaws at my core,
For the way I recoil from my own hands,
From the reflection that reminds me
Of everything I lack,
Everything I'll never be,
And the legacy of pain I wear
Like a brand,
His cruelty woven into my bones.

And I wonder, in this quiet hatred,
If I am doomed to this face,
This stranger's eyes,
This vessel I can't escape,
Forever haunted by the sight of myself,
Unloved, unworthy, unredeemable,
Bearing the spoils of a life I never chose,
A shadow I cannot break.

Story for the Blind

Braille on my skin
Telling the story
Of a thousand tragedies
Written in crimson ink.
By sharpened steel
A reminder that happy endings
Are for fairy tales.
And massage parlors

Patchwork

A patchwork of scars,
Unwanted, discarded,
Stretching across skin like memories
I'd rather forget.
The mirror reflects a story
I never wanted to tell.

Like Diogenes Discarding his Cup, I Dispose of my Blade.

I retired my blade,
Laid it down like a soldier's weapon,
No longer feeling worthy of the precision,
The clean split of cold steel against flesh.
Now I settle for tearing old wounds open,
Fingernails prying scabs
That cling to my skin like forgotten promises.

I peel each scar, layer by layer,
Feeling the brittle crack of dried blood breaking,
The raw sting of skin separating from itself.
There is no clean line now,
Only ragged edges,
Only the tearing,
The ache as blood rises,
Slow and familiar,
Spreading warmth along veins
That have longed for release.

I let the wounds weep,
Watch as old pain pools and spills anew,
As if my body still remembers the comfort
Of red rivers flowing, of hurt unbound.
This ritual of reopening, of tearing myself
Back to the beginning,
Is all I have left of the control I once held,
The precision I no longer deserve.

Salvation of Salt in the Wound

Caustic rain drops fall from my sleepless eyes
Diluting the rich crimson tracks upon my
Tattered thighs
Is this what is meant by washing away sins?
Or just extra punishment caused by saltwater
Tears which burn and sting?

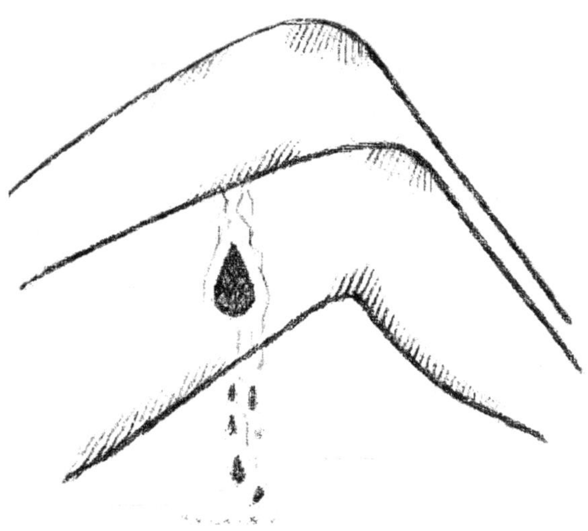

So Many Razor Blades, for Someone with a Beard

There was a time when reaching for a blade
Meant smoothing out the rough edges,
A quiet refinement –
An act of gentle control,
Trimming away excess,
Like pruning back,
The parts that no longer served.

Reaching for a glass meant a warmth spreading,
From the inside out,
A small rebellion,
A freedom poured in amber waves,
A taste that felt like laughter,
Like ease.

Pills were a kindness,
A way to mend,
Little capsules of relief,
Cradled in white plastic,
Promises wrapped in tiny shells,
And you –
You were the light that found its way in,
The warmth flooding my edges,
A cure I'd never named.

Bun now, the blade whispers differently –
Its touch is a scream buried in skin,

Self-Harm and Self-Worth

Tracing jagged paths like lightning veins,
Demanding more,
Taking more,
Leaving pieces that don't fit back together.

And the glass is a hollow emptiness,
I pour into myself,
Burning down my throat,
Settling heavy in my bones,
A quiet undoing with every swallow,
Its warmth turned cold
Long before it reaches
My heart.
Pills no longer soothe;
They sit heavy,
Foreign,
Weights pressing into my chest,
Little capsules of silence
That number,
But never heal,
Never touch the wound beneath.

And you –
You are a scar that won't fade,
A memory lodged like splinters under my skin,
A ghost that sits in the quiet hours,
Eyes hollow,
Watching as I reach
For the things that once brought life
But now only keep me alive.

The Stranger in the Mirror, Staring back with Disdain

I stand before the mirror,
A warped reflection staring back,
And all I see is wrong.
The face—a jigsaw of flaws, misfit pieces,
Eyes too hollow, nose too sharp,
A jawline carved from all the wrong angles,
Like someone sketched me once,
Then left the lines unfinished,
Left the edges too jagged, too raw.

My hair hangs like a shadow,
A color that doesn't belong,
Strands spilling down,
Fighting the shape of me, refusing to settle,
An alien weight I carry
But can't own, can't recognize.
It drapes over a body I don't know,
Don't want, don't want to touch,
Flesh that clings to bone,
Padding the places I hate to look at,
A thickness around the edges
Where I ache to be thin,
To disappear into something softer,
To erase the parts of me that refuse to fade.

I see scars on my legs,
Pale and purple lines that remember too much,

Self-Harm and Self-Worth

A map of past wounds,
Each one a reminder that I am marked,
That I am not clean,
Not whole,
That my skin is a canvas I can't scrape bare.
The tattoos, once bold, now faded,
Blurred like the memories I try to hold onto,
Yet slipping further away,
Leaving shadows where color once lived.

I despise this flesh, this unwanted vessel,
A shape I did not choose,
One I am forced to carry like a burden,
Dragging it through days and mirrors,
A weight that suffocates,
That never lightens.
I am trapped inside it,
This cage of flaws and scars,
Bound to the image I loathe,
To a face that feels borrowed,
To a body I cannot love,
Cannot forgive,
A body that fights me at every turn,
Mocking the softness I crave,
Denying me the peace of belonging.

In the glass, I am a stranger,
Something wrong from the start,
A figure carved by someone

Who looked away too soon,
Leaving only fragments in their wake.
And here I stand, despising each one,
Choking on the sight of myself,
Wishing, somehow,
To peel it all away,
To find something underneath
That I could look at without turning away.

Self-Sabotage of Self Medicated Shame (Unprescribed)

I close my eyes, fingers tracing
The raised memories of pain,
Littered across my body,
Hidden shamefully from sight.

I learned young to avoid the arms,
Or hands, to keep it above the knee,
Below the waist,
Out of the eyes of those around me –
My secret shame, my silent addiction.

These scars are reflections of pain,
Etched into what I call my skin,
Reminders of weakness carved deep,
Advertisements of my inability
To cope, to manage, to endure.

It's a cycle, this self-sabotage –
Scars feeding shame, and shame birthing scars,
Broken only by liquor
Or pills,
Trading the wounds of my skin,
For the slow disease inside.

Self-medicated, unprescribed,
Each swallow, each sting a prophecy,
An overdose written in the stars,
The method yet unknown,
But the ending already decided.

[105]

The Roots Within

I gaze down
And see roots of trees breaking through
The surface of my skin –
Years of growth pushing forward
Through harsh winters,
Through blissful summers,
Seasons shifting, but the roots remain,
Endlessly growing.

Roots of all colors –
The red of the new,
The purple of old –
Each a story,
A chapter penned in the book of my skin,
My life.

Some storylines forgotten,
Others as vivid as scenes from a film.
And like leaves that fall but roots that remain,
These stories are anchored deep, unchanging,
Each scar a whisper, a line penned in ink,
A reminder of paths I never chose to erase.

Section 5: Depression and Despair

Depression is a fog that lingers, dulling the senses and weighing down the soul. It's the silent companion that blurs the world, making even the brightest days feel hollow. In this section, despair becomes a quiet storm, a relentless force that pulls one under. These poems are an intimate glimpse into the shadowed spaces of the mind, where hope feels distant, and existence itself is questioned.

Graffiti Sleep: Exit Life Through the Gift Shop

I feel the sunlight brush against my eyelids,
Its light spilling across my face like paint from a
Careless hand, sneaking in through the cracks of
My window, uninvited, unrelenting.
It enters like an intruder with a spray can,
Fingers clenched around dawn's colors,
Tagging the Inside of my eyelids,
Waking me to graffiti I never asked for-
Bright strokes slashing through what little peace
The night offered.
I open my eyes,
Marked by morning's art,
Streaked with the weight of another day,
The soft vandalism of light spilled
Across my skin, an unwelcome reminder
That I'm still here.
Every morning,
I labor to scrub away the stain it leaves,
Each beam another task,
A weary fight against the brightness
I never asked to bear.

Maybe next time,
The night will finish what it started,
I'll no longer wake to this canvas of light,
This paint I never wanted.

Please, Omit Cruel Demons

This is the illness no one sees,
Pure OCD—the silent, relentless gnawing,
A sickness that sits quietly under my skin,
Its hands around my throat,
Its voice a quiet poison,
Dripping thoughts I cannot control,
Visions like shadows clawing their way up,
Insisting on truths I cannot bear to believe.

It tells me I am dark at the core,
That my mind is a stain that cannot be scrubbed,
And I wonder, am I only what it says?
These thoughts, these twisted glimpses,
Arrive unbidden,
Each one more vile than the last,
A secret horror whispered in my own voice.

I scrub my mind raw, try to wash it clean,
But the thoughts return, sharp and unwelcome,
Reminding me of their permanence,
That this is the price of breathing.
I am haunted by questions I didn't ask to own,
Visions I didn't invite,
Each one planting seeds of doubt
That grow like weeds in my chest,
Until I can't tell where I end
And the illness begins.

Depression and Despair

The world sees my steady hands,
My calm smile,
But underneath,
I am a tangle of fears,
Each one more grotesque than the last,
And I am left picking through the pieces,
Wondering if they are mine or something else,
If there's a difference at all.

I look in the mirror and see nothing whole,
Only fragments reflecting back,
A patchwork stitched from dread and disbelief,
The quiet scream of wanting to be clean,
To be rid of these thoughts
That cling like shadows,
To know who I am without them.

This is Pure OCD,
The illness that wears my face,
Its voice a thread woven into my own,
And I am left in the silence after it speaks,
Wondering if the sickness will ever let me go,
Or if I am doomed to carry this darkness,
Forever doubting the light in me.

Silent Colors and Empty Shells

Depression is the color of stillness,
A silent weight pressing down,
An invisible gravity that fills the room,
Sinking into every breath,
Turning air thick as tar,
Heavy as regret.
It is a garden left untended,
Where once-bright blooms curl inward,
Petals bruised and rotting at the edges,
Each leaf a memory forgotten,
Each stem reaching for a sun it can't feel,
A light that seems worlds away.

Inside me, there are doors shut tight,
Rooms I dare not enter,
Where shadows sit heavy on every surface,
Their outlines soft yet unyielding,
Like ghosts woven into wallpaper,
Waiting patiently to be seen,
But never calling out.

My thoughts drift like ash,
Cold embers of things I once loved,
Their edges crumbling as I try to hold them,
Slipping between my fingers,
Fading into dust that clings to my skin,
A residue of something lost,
Something I can no longer name.

Depression and Despair

There is a taste in my mouth,
Metallic and bitter,
Like pennies held too
Long between teeth,
A reminder of what it means to endure,
To swallow back the ache,
To sit with the hollowness
And pretend it isn't there.

Some days,
I am a cracked vessel,
Leaking quietly,
Slow drops of myself
Pooling at my feet,
Until I am hollow, empty,
An echo of something
That once was whole,
A shell that holds nothing
But the memory of hands
That once tried to mend it.

Depression is both vast and narrow,
An ocean and a cage,
A hunger that eats from the inside out,
Leaving me here, fragile and worn,
Waiting for the day when the weight lifts,
Or else presses so deep
That I simply dissolve,
Vanishing into the quiet,
One last breath against the stillness.

Bruised and Beaten before Breakfast, What's for Lunch?

Even as I open my eyes,
The dawn's light barely breaking the darkness,
I feel the weight of your words,
Sharp and cold as bone,
Their knuckles raw,
Each syllable a fist,
Raining down in hateful bursts,
Hailstones heavy with hurt,
Striking places unseen,
Leaving bruises that bloom in hidden colors,
Aching beneath the fragile surface of my skin.

Your words land with a relentless force,
Like stones cast from a hand
That knows no mercy,
Piercing the thin shelter I've tried to build,
My defenses crumbling
Under the weight of their impact.
They find every crack, every seam,
Seeping into wounds
That had only just begun to close,
Reopening each one with a bitterness
That stings deeper than the coldest winter air.

I carry these bruises like secrets,
Pressed into my bones,

Depression and Despair

Tucked away from sight,
Their pain a silent ache I wear quietly,
A mosaic of hurt blooming beneath
Where no one can see but me.
Each word you've thrown clings to my ribs,
Etching itself in invisible ink,
A language of sorrow
I've come to know by heart,
Its verses whispered in the dark,
Where the light dares not touch.

And still, as the storm of your words subsides,
I feel their echo, the tremor of each insult,
Settling like dust on my chest,
A residue of hurt that refuses to be swept away.
Even as I breathe, they linger, heavy as regret,
Filling my lungs with sorrow,
A weight pressing down, sinking deeper,
Until I wonder if I will ever rise
Unburdened by the bruises you leave behind,
Or if I am destined to wear them,
Silently, always,
A fragile vessel of wounds that will never heal

Motivated to Stay Down

What's the point in getting up,
When the ground always waits
Like a cruel lover beneath me,
Arms open wide for my fall?
Each time I rise, it pulls me back
Into the dirt, whispers of defeat
Seeping through the cracks.

How many times can I break
Before the pieces no longer fit.
Before I decide there's nothing left
But the weight of another knockdown,
Another stumble,
Another bruise.

What's the point in getting up,
When the world feels like a fist
And I'm always on the other end?
I used to stand because I believed
There was something left to stand for –
Hope, love, a dream too distant to see.

But now, I stand
Because it's all I've ever known,
Because somewhere in the silence,
Even if I can't hear it,
There's still a small voice
Telling me to try one more time.

But I cannot stand forever.

Cascading Sand of Relentless Time

I am an hourglass,
Fragile glass skin,
Cradling grains of coarse sand,
My life slipping downward,
Slow but certain,
Each speck a moment slipping away,
A quiet rush I feel but cannot see.

Sometimes I am tilted,
Rocked to the edge,
Close to tipping,
To halting this flow
Of life that drains relentlessly
Through me.
A surge of weight shifts within,
The grains heavy as regret,
Pressing against the thin wall
Of my skin.

I've thought of tipping myself,
Of shattering this vessel,
Spilling the sand that anchors me to time,
To breath,
To a heartbeat still pushing
Against the weight of its own ache.
I imagine the silence,
The stillness,
An end to the ceaseless fall of grains.

But then,
In some breathless pause,
I feel the faint stirring within me,
The grit of sand that has yet to settle,
The weight of life that remains.
Even in this slow descent,
There is something in me that holds,
Something that chooses not to fall.

And so I stand,
Glass unbroken,
Bearing the weight of every grain,
The fragile, delicate burden of being,
Letting time flow through me,
As I remain,
Whole in my waiting,
My life still ticking grain by grain.

Whiskey-Soaked Breath of Depression

It's always there —
A shadow in my steps, trailing close,
Growing darker when things are brightest.
It whispers my name in daylight,
Drunk on sorrow,
Hands stained with despair.

In the dark, it fades, melts into night,
But I feel it breathing,
Heavy, whiskey-soaked breath in my ear,
Pills rattling, knife-edge promises,
It moves with me, a weight, a shroud,
Silent, vast, and aching
As I carry its burden, it carries me.

Internal Rot, Exterior Decay

It begins in whispers,
Hairline cracks spidering across my skin,
The first tremors barely felt,
As if my bones themselves
Are holding their breath.
A heart shifts imperceptibly,
Quietly setting into decay,
Time etching its signature in dust
And ruin.

Pieces of me loosen
Like forgotten teeth,
Grain crumbling at the edges,
Each fragment a small rebellion
Against what holds it,
Each splinter a silent cry for release.
Memories root in the gaps,
Their weight patient but relentless,
Splitting foundations, prying open wounds
That once held firm against the world.

Eyes dull, clouded like old glass,
Webbed in fractures that catch the light,
Casting a mosaic of broken reflections
Across a mind choked
With ash and remnants.
Thoughts sag under the weight of regret,
A slow surrender to the pull of time,

Depression and Despair

My spirit bowing like weary shoulders.

Strength gives way in pieces,
One layer at a time,
Until all that remains
Is the bare skeleton of what I once was,
An empty ribcage open to the sky,
As if reaching upward for breath,
For the light I can no longer hold back.

And finally, I collapse,
A hushed exhalation,
A settling of dust,
The last trace of form
Slipping into formlessness,
Hope melting into earth,
Bones into fragments
Too small to see,
The structure unmade in silence,
Leaving only a scar of memory
Where I once dared to stand.

Go to Sleep under a Blanket of Fog

There was a time this mind was a forest,
Luch and green, paths well-worn
Where sunlight slipped through leaves
And dappled the ground like laughter,

Now, fog settles in, thick and clinging,
Wrapping around every tree,
Suffocating branches once alive with color.
I stumble over roots that weren't there before,
And the sky –
The sky has disappeared, replaced
By an endless ceiling of grey.

Nothing breathes here, not anymore,
The air is damp, heavy, every step a drag.
My feet sink deeper into the soil,
The weight of unseen things,
Pulling me down.

I wander without purpose,
Without direction,
Lost in a place I thought I knew.
The trees seem taller, darker,
And the light that once guided me
Is swallowed whole.

Here, in this forest of fog,
Even my own voice sounds foreign,

Depression and Despair

Muted by the mist,
My thoughts mere whispers
Swallowed by the silence.
I reach out,
But there is no path, no hand,
Only shadows that linger
And fade
As I sink further into the grey.

Beneath my Icy Exterior is a Churning Ocean

There is an ocean beneath this skin,
Vast and churning, hidden under a
Shell of ice.
The surface is calm, unbroken,
A pale sheet that stretches
Endlessly,
Reflecting the world back,
Hard and cold.

Beneath, the water roars,
But no one can hear it –
The waves crash in silence,
Swallowed by the thick ice above,
Trapped in a space where sound
Cannot reach.

I pound against the surface,
Fists numb from the cold,
From trying to break through
To something warm,
Something that feels real.
But the ice does not crack;
It only stares back,
My face warped in its cold reflection,
A stranger in my own skin.

This weight bears down,

Depression and Despair

Relentless,
Pressing the life
From my lungs,
Stealing breath after fetid breath,
Until I am still,
Frozen beneath the surface,
A silent scream
Caught in the glassy depths.

Inside, the ocean waits,
Restless,
A pulse beneath the numbness,
A storm yearning
For release.
But the world sees only the ice,
Unbroken,
And I am left alone
In this frozen quiet,
An ocean too deep
For anyone to reach.

Happy Hollow Halloween

Every day is Halloween here,
My mask pulled tight, grinning
A plastic smile that stretches too far,
Cracks at the edges,
A façade thin as paper,
Hiding the hollow beneath.

I am a patchwork stitched by habit –
Depression sewn into the seams,
Addiction stitched over bruised veins,
Heartbreak pressing down, heavy as stone,
Filling the cavity where a heart used to beat.

They say Halloween is for ghosts,
For the restless dead who walk among us,
But I am the dead, standing here,
Moving through days like a shadow cast
Without substance or shape.

And the world around me plays along,
Ignoring the empty spaces in my eyes,
Laughing at the costume I wear –
The "normal" I pretend to be,
My voice practiced into words
That mean nothing but sound real enough.

It's the day of the dead, and I walk with them
Familiar with the quiet between breaths,

Depression and Despair

With the ache that presses cold
Against my skin.
I am alive only as far as this mask allows,
This cheap trick of pretending to live,
To smile, to laugh, to belong.

Beneath, I am bone and dust,
A whisper of what I once was,
An echo waiting for silence,
While the mask I wear holds my place,
Plays my part in a life I no longer feel.
Every day, I paint it on,
And every night, I peel it off
To see the hollow skull beneath,
The truth of this haunted thing I am –
Just another ghost in a costume,
Drifting through, waiting
To disappear.

Always a Chair, Never a Seat

I am the faulty office chair,
Always sinking, always down,
Wheels skewed, a crooked dance,
Unable to find the straight, clear path.

My fabric frayed, seams undone,
Edges bare, with stuffing exposed,
A seat forgotten in the corners dust,
Silently holding the weight of being left.

And here I sit, still bearing the sign –
Labelled with a single word,
Damaged
As if it's all I am.

Yet, even broken, I am here,
Threadbare, tilted, wheels misaligned,
Holding the shape of those who stayed
Just long enough to leave their mark.

Reflection of Ruins

I look in the mirror, see a monster stare back,
A twisted wreck of flesh, a grotesque attack.
Every inch a betrayal, every glance a curse,
No matter the numbers, it only gets worse.

Digits lie-
They whisper sweet deceit,
but I see the truth rotting beneath my feet.
Fat, flesh, failure wrapped in a skin too tight,
Stretched over bones that should feel light.

Hunger gnaws, yet I refuse to eat,
Each pang a weakness, each bite a defeat.
Bones should show, ribs should rise,
But all I see is the bloated disguise.

I wear this ugliness like a second skin,
Trapped in this form, no way to begin.
A prison of fat, of shame, of hate,
No diet, no effort, can change this fate.

I loathe the sight, despise the feel,
No scale or compliment can make it real.
I'm drowning in layers; I can't peel away-
The ugliness remains and will always stay.

Section 6: Suicide and Finality

When darkness becomes unbearable, thoughts of escape can feel like the only path to peace. This section confronts the heaviest moments, the contemplation of letting go and the search for release from suffering. It is a space for those final thoughts, the raw honesty of a soul seeking silence. These poems offer a haunting glimpse into the edge of existence, a testament to the resilience found even in the act of survival.

One Last Tequila Slammer, for the Road

Shot by shot,
I swallowed the dark.
Tequila burning through
Broken veins.
I laid down, too tired to stand,
Head covered in plastic,
Helium hissing like a final lullaby.
Couldn't place the smell at first,
Or from where it came –
And when I did,
I smiled,
Lemon scented trash bags –
Eyes closing, ready to leave behind
The tears that tasted like salt
And regret.

Ever Present

Death surrounds me –
Family, pet, love –
Tormenting me with their presence,
Then taken away.
Teasing me with the inevitable march
To nothingness

It sounds so peaceful,
To cease to exist,
No more pain,
No more misguided hope –
Just silence,
Pain-free,
Calm.

Realization

Realizing you're gone,
Though you remain – I see you, we talk,
Yet the part of you that was ours
Has departed

Realizing this pain
Is now forever mine,
As constant as breathing,
Or what's left of my heart beating.

Realizing that intoxication
Only momentarily numbs,
Before the ache returns,
Sharper than before.

Realizing there's only one way
To silken the pain, to end the ache;
Euthanize my heart, take it from me –
It belongs to you and always will.

Realizing that to live
Without love,
Without you,
Is death.

Realizing what I must do….

Swallowed by Fog

When all you see ahead of you is loneliness,
Like a fog swallowing the path,
Let the quiet hold you.
Each step, a small echo in the hollow night,
Whispering you are not alone.

From A to Z, Fuck the Rest

We are birthed,
Purely to die –
I'm just cutting out the middleman
Called Life.

Closing Note

Thank you for taking the time to journey through these pages with me. Your presence here, as a reader, is deeply appreciated. Poetry has a way of reaching into the heart's quiet corners, and I hope these words offered you a space to reflect, to feel, or simply to be.

If you've ever felt compelled to write, let this be an invitation—try your hand at poetry. Words have power, whether whispered, written, or shouted into the night. Or, if you feel this book speaks to someone else you know, please share it; sometimes, knowing others have walked similar paths can make all the difference.
Above all, remember that life, with all its trials, sometimes hides reasons to carry on in the smallest, most unexpected places.

The human body and mind are wired to want to survive and will find that small reason somewhere. The first time I planned to kill myself, my dog wouldn't stop barking at me or biting at my feet as I tried to leave the house. Looking back, I could have locked her in the kitchen or another room in the house, but it never crossed my mind at the time. So, I sat, back to the door holding that precious pup, crying. If not for her, I would not be here.

[135]

The second time I tried to kill myself, I had my head in a trash bag taped at one end to a helium tank and as the hiss of the helium started to fill the bag, the overwhelming smell of artificial lemons from the scented bag got to me and I stopped (this is the basis for the poem *One Last Tequila Slammer, for the Road)*, again, I could have just gone with it, but that overwhelming survival instinct can be found in the most simple of things.

Even when the weight feels too heavy, hold on. That tiny glimmer, however faint, might just be the light you need. Never give up—you are not alone. Thank you, once again, for being part of this story.

Thank you,

-Edgar J. Wilde

www.EdgarJWilde.com

www.ingramcontent.com/pod-product-compliance
Lightning Source LLC
Chambersburg PA
CBHW070906160726
48004CB00003B/1257